GATES *of* HARVARD YARD

GATES OF HARVARD YARD

EDITED WITH AN INTRODUCTION BY

Blair Kamin

Essays by Ariana Austin, Gokcan Demirkazik,
Jeneen Interlandi, Blair Kamin,
Becca Mazur, Kathy Ran, Melissa Simonetti,
Licia Sky, Lily Sugrue, Ola Topczewska,
and Rachel Wehr

FOREWORD BY ANN MARIE LIPINSKI

PHOTOGRAPHS BY RALPH LIEBERMAN
SKETCHES BY ROGER ERICKSON
MAP BY CHRISTOPHER BECK

PRINCETON ARCHITECTURAL PRESS · NEW YORK

CONTENTS

Northwest Gates

THE CLASS OF 1881 GATE

THE CLASS OF 1876 (HOLWORTHY)

THE CLASS OF 1886 GATE

THE CLASS OF 1870 GATE

THE CLASS OF 1874 GATE

JOHNSTON GATE

THE CLASS OF 1875 GATE

THE CLASS OF 1857 GATE

McKEAN (PORCELLIAN CLUB) GATE

THE CLASS OF 1889 GATE

MORGAN (CLASS OF 1877) GATE

DEXTER (CLASS OF

South & Southwest Gates

OF 1879) GATE

ADSTREET GATE

THE CLASSES OF 1887 AND 1888 GATE

THE FIRE STATION GATE

North Gates

ROBINSON GATE

THE CLASS OF 1885 GATE

EMERSON GATE

ELIOT (CLASS OF 1908) GATE

LOEB HOUSE GATE

17 QUINCY DRIVE GATE

LAMONT LIBRARY GATE

SITE OF DEMOLISHED
DUDLEY MEMORIAL GATE

LAMONT DELIVERY GATE

ON (CLASS OF 1880) GATE

East Gates

Unlocking the Story of the Gates

BY ANN MARIE LIPINSKI

The gates that Pulitzer Prize-winning critic Blair Kamin examines in this book are of the physical kind—iron, stone, and brick sentries surrounding one of the world's great universities. But there is another gate documented within these pages: the invisible passage through which Kamin and a group of Harvard students passed in search of a story about architecture and ambition never fully told.

That quest began when Kamin arrived on the Harvard campus in the fall of 2012 to begin his Nieman Fellowship, a year of study awarded to some of the world's most promising journalists. Kamin is an architecture critic who pays deep attention to the ways in which design and the built environment shape and influence our lives, a writer with the power to make observations that stick. I have been reading Blair for many years and often find my travels framed by his lens. I cannot pass Harvard's beloved Memorial Hall, built in the 1870s, without recalling his description of its elaborate topknot as a "Victorian riot," or attend a concert at Chicago's Frank Gehry-designed Pritzker Pavilion without thinking of its fluttering curled canopy as "Betty Boop's eyelashes." But Kamin's gifts surpass lively metaphor to render even the most familiar environments in new and provocative ways. In awarding him the prize

OPPOSITE: Students and visitors pass through Johnston Gate, the main entrance to Harvard Yard. In the background is a familiar scene: tourists snapping photographs of the John Harvard statue.

for criticism, the Pulitzer Board highlighted not only Kamin's lucid style, but also his work that poses hard questions about equality and fairness in the way we develop and build.

Each Nieman Fellow, like each Harvard student, comes to campus with a special set of interests and skills. Kamin's drew him to the Graduate School of Design, where he found faculty and course work to deepen his knowledge and criticism. But the campus itself beckoned as a laboratory, and what began as research into Harvard's architectural history soon evolved to focus on the legacy of the twenty-five gates that rim Harvard Yard. His review of the literature affirmed a belief that a full account of the story behind the gates had not been written. By the end of his first semester, he was preparing a syllabus and a plan to train his critic's eye on the gates as a means of teaching critical thinking, arts journalism, photography, and historic research. That winter, along with Nieman Fellows Jeneen Interlandi and Finbarr O'Reilly, Kamin led Harvard students on an architectural expedition that wended its way through every gate as well as the archival records documenting their provenance and construction. The results yielded wonderful stories of each gate's unique identity, tales that paint a nuanced portrait of not just Harvard, but also some of the individuals and ambitions that helped shape its identity. The class also documented deteriorating conditions at several of the gates, information that inspired alumni to contribute to enhancements at the Johnston Gate of 1889, the first built at Harvard. Kamin continued work on the project long after the class ended, and the result is this book.

As a writer and editor, I'm attracted to the stories we find in the quiet places. *Gates of Harvard Yard* is an architecture critic's version of that, an examination not of the bustling Yard or the iconic edifices defining this campus, America's first. Kamin instead animates the often-forgotten passages that every day guide thousands in and out of the university's well-trafficked public spaces. He writes that "understanding Harvard Yard's overlooked edge is essential to grasping its celebrated center," a worthy framing not only for this undertaking but also for any analysis of public space.

What ultimately inspires Kamin is the idea that a gate is indeed a physical thing, but also an aspiration—of beginning, of belonging, of entry into something bigger than oneself. "Enter to Grow in Wisdom," reads the inscription on the Dexter Gate, an invitation Kamin embraced. In reading this critic's meditation on the gates, it is that promise that lingers, the one so movingly celebrated by the great poet Seamus Heaney in "Villanelle for an Anniversary," written to mark Harvard's 350th. It ends:

Begin again where frosts and tests were hard.
Find yourself or founder. Here, imagine
A spirit moves, John Harvard walks the yard,
The books stand open and the gates unbarred.

Entering to Grow in Wisdom and Delight

BY BLAIR KAMIN

All too often, the gates that herald the entrance to Harvard Yard are seen (if they are seen at all) as architectural afterthoughts. Harried students, professors, and visitors rush through these portals, treating them as mere passageways that lead to grand edifices, not carefully wrought constructions that direct human movement and uplift everyday experience. This guidebook urges a different view: Pause. Behold. And see these elegant, often magnificent, sentries with fresh eyes.

The twenty-five portals form a legacy that is rich in architectural artistry and the lore of a renowned university. Despite their aura of architectural permanence, they open a window onto Harvard's shifting aspirations and identity—from its origins as a tiny all-male training ground for Puritan ministers to a sprawling institution that percolates many of the world's great ideas and draws students from every strata of society. Yet the complete story of the gates has never been fully told. This book endeavors to fill that gap, revealing how remarkable architects, visionary patrons, and generous classes of alumni joined forces to transform Harvard Yard's perimeter and, with it, the university's architectural character.

OPPOSITE: The traditional design of the Meyer Gate at once frames a view of Harvard's Science Center and exhibits a study in contrast with its modern architecture.

Principally made of brick, stone, and wrought iron, the gates belong to a global phenomenon as old as time. From the imposing entrance to Beijing's Forbidden City to the triumphal passageway of Berlin's Brandenburg Gate to the glistening Gateway Arch in Saint Louis, human beings have been building gates for millennia. The reasons transcend geography and cultural differences. Gates control access and keep out those who are considered dangerous or undesirable. They are expressions of power and prestige as well as anxiety and conflict. They incite emotions ranging from awe to trepidation. That is because they often mark crucial transitions, from life to death, as at the entrances to cemeteries, or from ignorance to wisdom, as at the portals of universities. They have inspired artists who portray them as thresholds to transcendent realms (most famously, Lorenzo Ghiberti in the *Gates of Paradise* and Auguste Rodin in *The Gates of Hell*). Seen in this light, gates do not simply delineate space; they communicate ideals and serve as symbols of human aspiration, even divine order. Whatever motivates their construction, they are ubiquitous—so much so that it can be said without great exaggeration that there are three certainties in life: death, taxes, and gates. Like Janus, the Roman god of beginnings and transitions, gates are profoundly ambiguous and complex, rather like life itself. And if there is an afterlife, we will, as some believe, encounter gates there too.

Harvard Yard's gates have a story all their own. On a campus that will celebrate its four-hundredth anniversary in 2036, these proud portals are relative newcomers. Harvard began raising them in the late 1880s to replace a simple post-and-rail fence that had surrounded the Yard since colonial times. The first of the new passageways was the majestic Johnston Gate of 1889 by architect Charles Follen McKim of McKim, Mead & White. It eschewed Victorian clutter and returned Harvard to its colonial-era, Georgian design roots. Following Johnston Gate's template of variegated "Harvard brick" and intricate webs of wrought iron, two subsequent building campaigns—one in the twentieth century's first decade and the other in 1936 when Harvard celebrated its three-hundredth anniversary, or

ABOVE: The classically inspired details of the Class of 1889 Gate harmonize perfectly with Wigglesworth Hall's dormer windows and teeth-like dentils.

Tercentenary—erected other gates and fences to form Harvard Yard's distinctive enclosure.

The new gates were at once protective and welcoming. On one hand, they cloistered the contemplative parklike Yard from the urban tumult exemplified by the trolleys that once rumbled through Harvard Square. In the same vein, they limited access to the Yard, a function that drew criticism in 2011 when Harvard used them to restrict entrance to people with university IDs because of security concerns prompted by the tent encampment of the Occupy Harvard movement. Yet with many Yard buildings turning inward to the campus rather than outward to the street, the gates became the face of Harvard, lending its imposing buildings a much-needed human scale.

In keeping with urban planning's City Beautiful movement, they also concealed Harvard's architectural hodgepodge of clashing styles—Georgian, Federal, Victorian, and Beaux-Arts—behind a unifying neo-Georgian scrim.

While several of the gates were chiefly sponsored by individual patrons—ambassadors, captains of industry, and titans of Wall Street—most were funded by classes of Harvard alumni. This continued a tradition of class-based giving that began with the stained-glass windows in Memorial Hall, the university's High Victorian Gothic tribute to the Harvard men who fought on the Union side in the Civil War. The myriad mysterious numbers that adorn the gates and their adjoining fences are actually tributes to the classes that raised money for

ABOVE: The wrought-iron filigree of the Class of 1870 Gate frames a view of Holden Chapel's ornate blue gable.

the passageways. In current dollars, their total cost is conservatively estimated at nearly $3.5 million. Their architectural and urban design value, however, is priceless—enough to counter the often-voiced criticism that they form an intimidating barrier between town and gown.

Unlike Yale's walled Collegiate Gothic quadrangles, Harvard Yard's enclosure strikes an alluring balance between the opposing traditions of the fortified enclosure and the open New England common. Spear-tip finials and a virtual menagerie of aggressive animals rendered in stone—eagles, lions, and rams—express the martial impulse. Nature is celebrated in an array of wrought-iron leaves and flowers that echo the gnarly branches and stark tracery of the Yard's elm trees. At the same time, the see-through quality of the adjoining fences allows passersby to enjoy the Yard's pastoral presence. The gates, in short, are both militaristic and naturalistic. They don't simply enclose the Yard. They engage it. And their influence reaches far beyond the heart of Harvard's campus, an impact evident in the neo-Georgian architecture of such prominent buildings as the cupola-topped dormitories along the Charles River. All have their own impressive gates.

Even so, as a team of Harvard students discovered during the 2013 Wintersession class that led to this book, some of the Harvard Yard gates are victims of neglect. A few are needlessly locked. Others are being allowed to fall apart. Still others are marred by third-rate landscaping. Many are improperly referred to on campus maps and in media accounts—not by their donors' names, but by the names of nearby buildings. It's as though the gates are viewed as marginal because they delineate the spaces leading to such monumental buildings as the Beaux-Arts Widener Library.

In reality, as the following pages show, understanding Harvard Yard's overlooked edge is essential to grasping its celebrated center. While many other American universities boast proud gates, Harvard's ensemble is preeminent. To pause and behold the gates of Harvard Yard is to see them through a new prism, one that frames a richer, deeper view of Harvard's history, identity, and beauty.

Harvard Yard's Oldest and Grandest

BY OLA TOPCZEWSKA

Thousands of students and visitors pass through Harvard's Johnston Gate every day, but few look up long enough to fully appreciate this gate—the oldest, grandest, and most influential of all the gates surrounding Harvard Yard.

Built in 1889, this entrance remains the imposing centerpiece of Harvard Yard's 3,828-foot fenced enclosure. It marked an architectural turning point for the Yard and the end of an era of Victorian Gothic architecture exemplified by Memorial Hall. Its Georgian Revival design influenced the rest of the gates around the Yard, as well as buildings within and beyond it. The elegant River Houses, the serene enclave of the Harvard Business School, and the picturesque John W. Weeks Bridge spanning the Charles River all draw upon Johnston Gate's architectural DNA.

The gate's namesake, Samuel Johnston, who would go on to become a wealthy Chicago financier and real estate entrepreneur, left Harvard due to poor eyesight, and later returned to graduate in 1855. When Johnston walked the Yard, it was sectioned off by a rudimentary wooden fence, a structure that had served for centuries as its primary border. Both Johnston and the university deemed the fence unworthy of its setting. Upon his death in 1886, Johnston left Harvard $10,000 (about $250,000 in today's dollars) for the construction of a grand portal. The funds also backed fencing on the gate's flanks.

As designed by Charles McKim of the New York architectural firm McKim, Mead & White, whose best-known works include the Boston Public Library and New York's old Pennsylvania Station, the gate is stately and dignified. It has a recessed central entrance wide enough for a horse carriage, and two pedestrian gates on its flanks. Massive brick walls and piers frame its central feature, a visually stunning web of wrought iron that drove up the gate's cost by 60 percent. Atop the wrought iron is a cross, harkening back to Harvard's roots as a training ground for ministers, as well as the numbers "1636," recognizing the year of the university's founding, and a tiny shield inscribed with "1889," when the gate was completed.

McKim made the gate harmonious with the Yard's older buildings, especially the adjacent Massachusetts Hall of 1720, Harvard's oldest surviving building, and the cupola-topped Harvard Hall from 1766. To convey a sense of age, he looked for "culls," bricks that had

OVERLEAF: The main entrance to Harvard Yard, Johnston Gate, is framed by two of the university's oldest buildings, the cupola-topped Harvard Hall (left) and Massachusetts Hall. The U-shaped gate consists of a central carriage gate (now used by vehicles) and flanking foot gates.

been turned green, tan, or black by excessive heat. He asked masons to lay them out in a sophisticated pattern called Flemish bond, which showcased their variegated color. The unique style became known as "Harvard brick." The design so successfully wove the gate into the fabric of the university's architecture that McKim, a Harvard dropout, was awarded an honorary degree immediately after the gate's triumphal debut.

Johnston Gate is more than a portal; it serves as a memorial to Harvard's history. Its brick walls are relieved by stone tablets with inscriptions detailing the college's founding. Seals on the brick piers—one for Harvard, another for the state of Massachusetts, which helped fund the fledgling college—lend a sense of authority. On the side of the piers facing the Yard are Johnston's personal seal, including an eagle encircled by a wreath, and the seal of Cambridge, which portrays Harvard's now-demolished Gothic Revival Gore Hall.

Also visible on the Yard side of the gate are niches cut into its brick piers. One of the niches was originally fitted with a drinking fountain that also boasted a larger basin on the ground for horses and dogs. The other niche had no fountain but was fitted with a low bench. Today the water basins are filled with gravel, and the fountain runs no more.

Critics termed Johnston Gate a grandiose departure from Harvard's Puritan origins. Even before the gate's completion, McKim had to steady the hand of Harvard officials who were concerned by the project's ever-escalating cost.

"I feel that it is no time to be timid," he wrote to them. At the end of the typed letter, he added, in pen: "Believe me."

McKim's vision was salvaged by a donation from his sister-in-law, Mrs. George von L. Meyer of Boston. A small shield on the gate's Yard-facing side displays what appears to be the letters "AAM." They are actually meant to be read in reverse as

OPPOSITE: The Harvard shield, including the "Veritas" motto displayed on three open books, endows Johnston Gate with a sense of authority.

"MAA"—von L. Meyer's maiden name (Marian Alice Appleton). The year of Harvard's founding, 1636, also reads in reverse from the Yard side.

For decades the Johnston Gate was used for daily pedestrian access to the Yard and the rare passage of a ceremonial carriage. But in 1983 the gate became the Yard's main entry for cars and service vehicles. This required the construction of a gatehouse, a Victorian Gothic booth that set the university back $25,000 per square foot, making it Harvard's most expensive building on a per-square-foot basis. In 1992 Harvard completed a $3.5 million restoration of the Yard's gates and fencing, directed by Boston architect Michael Teller. The gates, including Johnston, were repainted with anticorrosive techniques developed for North Sea oil platforms.

Harvard made more improvements in 2014, the 125th anniversary of the gate's completion. Following a design by landscape architect Michael Van Valkenburgh, the university replaced two patches of dirt on the gate's Massachusetts Avenue side with swamp oak trees and liriope ground cover that blooms with violet flowers. The Harvard Club of Chicago, which takes great pride in the gate because Johnston called Chicago home, raised more than $7,000 for the project.

The landscaping reprises the gate's role as an entrance to, and an extension of, the Yard's greenery. As part of the changes, the university tucked a new feature beneath the surface—a nontoxic type of soil that creates its own nitrogen and has less need for water and fertilizer than ordinary dirt. This balancing act between tradition and innovation is appropriate for Johnston Gate, a vital and precedent-setting landmark that serves as one of Harvard's most public faces.

OPPOSITE, TOP: The array of wrought iron atop Johnston Gate includes a wreath-adorned cross that symbolizes Harvard's early commitment to training ministers as well as numerals denoting the year of the university's founding, 1636. Above "1636" is a small shield displaying the year of the gate's completion, 1889. OPPOSITE, BOTTOM: A Victorian Gothic gate house allows campus security to monitor vehicles passing through the entry into Harvard Yard.

Its Glory Was Fleeting

BY OLA TOPCZEWSKA

When Harvard's Class of 1874 Gate first swung open in 1901, it symbolized two things: the commitment and success of the graduates of 1874, and the design skills of McKim, Mead & White, the architectural firm that created this gate and most of the others surrounding the Yard. If the the class members of 1874 were still alive, they might be deeply disturbed to see what has become of their memorial.

Built for $4,482, roughly $105,000 in current dollars, the gate was the least expensive of a trio of portals completed in 1901. Yet its worth was much greater than this modest outlay. Like its sibling gates, which were donated by the classes of 1870 and 1886, the 1874 Gate played a critical role as an entrance to the Yard's northwest corner. The 1870 Gate, the center entryway and largest of the trio, opened onto the quiet courtyard of Holden Chapel. The 1886 Gate directed students into the courtyard fronted by Stoughton Hall. Likewise, the 1874 Gate led to the front door of Hollis Hall.

Despite limited funds, McKim, Mead & White effectively employed simple shapes, including ovals and rectangles, to create a complex and visually compelling structure. Many of the finer details are combinations of C- and S-shaped scrollwork, wrought carefully out of iron by master craftsmen. The gate's ironwork is bordered by two brick columns, designed to match the brick pattern of the colonial halls in Harvard Yard. Atop the gate's arch is a lantern, currently unused. The overall impression is one of elegance and sophistication.

Still, the tight budget prevented certain refinements. The gate's brick piers include two limestone tablets, perfect canvases for inscriptions that were never added. In contrast, inscriptions are present on the 1886 Gate, reflecting the fact that the class of 1886 donated more money for its entry.

Worse, a mere twenty-four years after the construction of the 1874 Gate, the money and thought invested into the gate were rendered useless. Lionel Hall, a freshman dormitory built in 1925, walled off the gate from the courtyard to which it once led. The gate was locked, and it has been inoperative since then. Views through the gate of the leafy courtyard within have been replaced by brick and mortar. The gate is now little more than a glorified fence.

The area outside the northwest corner of the Yard was struck another blow around 1970 with the construction of the Cambridge Street underpass, which funneled a constant stream of cars and trucks past the Yard and into an underground tunnel. This created a sense of

ABOVE: Richly sculpted wrought-iron ornament enlivens the Class of 1874 Gate.
OPPOSITE: The modest gate has been locked for decades.
The construction of Lionel Hall in 1925 walled off the gate from Harvard Yard,
rendering it obsolete.

commotion and generated noise pollution and glare outside the gate—hardly the type of setting envisioned by its designers.

Michael Booth, former proctor in Entryway A in Lionel Hall, lived in the suite that looks out on the back of the 1874 Gate. "I think it's a pleasant piece of scenery," said Booth, "but it's a little sad that the classes never know what the fate of their donations will be."

When it comes to preserving a legacy, even fashioning it out of brick and iron is no guarantee of immortality.

A "Secret Garden" Beckons

BY LILY SUGRUE

Mary Lennox, the little heroine of Frances Hodgson Burnett's *The Secret Garden*, unburied the key to her aunt's long-shuttered rose garden. She found the gate, pushed aside the ivy growing over it, turned the lock, and stepped inside. Then she brought the garden back to life.

At Harvard, tucked in the enclave between Mower and Lionel Halls and Holden Chapel, there exists a sort of secret garden. It too has a gate that is kept locked. No ivy grows over this gate; its key is not hidden away somewhere, and the "garden" behind—actually an intimate courtyard—can still be reached from the softly arched paths that curl around either side of the chapel. It is the gate that could use a Mary Lennox of its own to breathe some life back into it.

Designed by Charles McKim of McKim, Mead & White, the wrought-iron gate with its granite base and brick piers was erected in 1901 as the centerpiece of the architect's three-piece suite. It was constructed on an axis with what is now the back door of Holden Chapel (a new front door was built and the original facade of the chapel was duplicated in 1850). In the fence flanking the gate, the number 70 is set in metal circles at regular intervals. Both the gate and fencing were gifts to Harvard from the class of 1870.

The gate itself is an extraordinary confection, a wedding cake of wrought iron. Slender, black spear tips top the individual pickets. At the gate's center rises an anthemion, an elegant flourish of open petals. The fine detailing continues in the gate's supporting posts—rectangular

prisms ornamented with a careful combination of intricate scrollwork and floral details. The posts are topped by even more fanciful flourishes, including pineapple caps, a traditional symbol of welcome. Above, the central arch is deliberately elongated, allowing all of Holden to be seen through the gate. The effect is like an exquisite trim of wrought-iron lace, perfectly highlighting the chapel's ornate, sky blue pediment.

For all its multitudes of curlicues, the gate is not overdone. Unlike the Johnston or Meyer gates, the 1870 Gate is not monumental. It's human-scaled, and creates a lovely continuity between the creamy scrollwork and cherubs that frost the pediment of Holden Chapel. This gate was meant to be used, a quiet little delight for anyone willing to pay attention. And the curious onlookers who peek through the pickets will certainly be delighted—until they realize that the threshold is barred.

OVERLEAF: Located on the northwest side of Harvard Yard, the locked Class of 1870 Gate once led to Holden Chapel, visible in the background.

Behind the gate sits the secret "garden." When the class of 1870 gave the money for the fencing and the gate (at the time the gate cost $4,483, which would be worth at least $100,000 today), it also gave the gift of a sundial. A sensuous stone base sits on an unadorned octagonal pedestal nestled between the chapel and the gate. Around the base of the sundial, the words "On This Moment Hangs Eternity" are inscribed. The footpaths leave a little grassy lawn around the sundial as they make their way toward the gate from either side of the chapel. Branches extend overhead, forming a delicate canopy over this outdoor temple. The little quad is peaceful and secluded, managing to create a quiet space just off the hustle and bustle of Massachusetts Avenue.

But not all is well in the garden. Dark-green lichen creeps over the word "Eternity," darkening the white-gray stone. The face of the sundial has been rubbed bare by years of exposure. Its Roman numerals are barely discernible, but it doesn't matter. The sundial has not been readable since Lionel and Mower were constructed, blocking the sun and access to the Class of 1870's two sister gates.

At the base of the gate's post, tiny wrought-iron leaves have rusted and broken away. On the gate itself hangs a padlock with just the slightest chips of rust and black paint. The gate is always kept locked.

Surely this does not have to be. No, Lionel and Mower are not going to be moved and the dial will probably never again see the sun. But this gate can still be rescued.

Most other universities can only dream of owning a beautiful little space such as this. And yet, the 1870 Gate is left closed off to the world, its pieces falling apart. No part of McKim, Mead & White's dignified design, no matter how small, should be rusting away. Restore the little leaves, or, at the least, recoat and protect those that remain. Then take a lesson from Mary Lennox—open the gate and unlock its garden.

OPPOSITE: A sundial mounted on a curvaceous base graces
the courtyard framed by the Class of 1870 Gate. The inscription
on the base reads "On This Moment Hangs Eternity."

An Indelicate Fate

BY RACHEL WEHR

A filigree of floral finials and iron tendrils rises toward a tapered lantern topping the arch of the Class of 1886 Gate. It is a small Georgian garden of a gate, one that should invite students into the Holden Courtyard. But for decades, it has stood, bolted and rusting, against the cold back wall of Mower Hall.

In 1901 Harvard's gates sprang up like so many wrought-iron daisies. That year ten classes and the Porcellian Club answered President Charles William Eliot's call to give gates as gifts to the school. The class of 1886 spent $3,488 (which today would be worth at least $81,000) for a gate celebrating the fifteenth anniversary of their commencement. The Gate of 1886 was built as part of a suite of sentries lining Holden Courtyard, as a twin to the 1874 Gate and as a companion to a grander, more central 1870 Gate. And though parents should never choose a favorite child, architectural firm McKim, Mead & White made 1886 the more ornate and refined twin, since there was $300 more from the alumni to spend on the design. The alumni should have saved their money.

The class of 1886 had chosen the quiet northwest corner of Harvard Yard, opposite Stoughton Hall. The class secretary believed the site "especially good, not only because it is surrounded by a group of old buildings, but also because the open space in front makes certain an excellent distant view of the gate when completed." The courtyard was to be the focal point. The floral design recalled the Class Day exercises

that took place at Holden every year, where seniors traditionally wrestled over a wreath of flowers as their girls looked on.

It was a change in campus housing policies that sealed the gate's fate. In 1924 President A. Lawrence Lowell took a bold stance against the expensive "Gold Coast" dormitories edging Harvard Square and mandated that all Harvard freshmen live in the Yard. Twin dorms, Lionel and Mower Halls, were constructed near the gate to accommodate the freshmen. Together, the new buildings closed off the Old Yard as well as any fence could. Mower left just a narrow moat of grass between its back wall and the 1886 Gate. After only twenty-four years of use, its doors were closed and locked, its delicate wrought-iron flowers born to blush unseen from within the Yard.

Today instead of looking into the grand face of Stoughton and the calm reprieve of the courtyard, the 1886 Gate looks into a scene less serene: the room of the freshman living in Mower B-11.

ABOVE: An intricate wrought-iron flower, encircled by other
embellishments, appears against the backdrop of Mower Hall's brick walls.
OPPOSITE: Bright sun casts sharp shadows beyond the Class of 1886 Gate.
The building of Mower Hall in the 1920s blocked the gate.

Architects designed the dorms to be only two stories high out of
respect for the modest size of Holden Chapel; however, they showed
less respect for the gates and memorials surrounding the dorm. In 1925
a caretaker of the grounds did not mourn the loss long, saying that the
dial is "just as ornamental out of the sun as it was in, and about as useful." So too is the 1886 Gate relegated to a worn architectural flourish.

A Short-Lived Vision

BY JENEEN INTERLANDI

When members of the class of 1881 dedicated the gate in front of Phillips Brooks House at their twenty-fifth reunion, they articulated a simple if impossibly bold goal for the wrought-iron edifice: "that [it] shall express in the majesty of [its] simplicity at least this: the invitation which our beloved college offers to the youth of this wide land, to come within its gates, in order that in whole-hearted service to the truth, they may enter into life and so be free."

Were any of them alive today, they might be disappointed to know that their particular gate extended this invitation for just a short while (less than a century, in fact, which is nothing by the standards of a university founded in 1636). According to the house's operations manager, the portal has been locked for decades.

Both the gate and the house were named after the Reverend Phillips Brooks (class of 1855), a renowned preacher at Trinity Church in Boston, whose most noted accomplishments include writing the lyrics for the famous Christmas carol "O Little Town of Bethlehem" and inspiring the design of Trinity Church, an architectural triumph that contains the first freestanding liturgical altar in the United States. Such were the love and devotion of Brooks's patrons that, upon his death in 1893, close to six hundred people contributed to his memorial fund, raising a total of $71,046 (nearly $2 million in today's dollars)—enough to build a memorial house and establish an endowment for a charitable organization, the Phillips Brooks House Association.

For the gate, the class of 1881 raised an additional $5,000, worth at least $115,000 today.

The house and gate were designed by Alexander Wadsworth Longfellow Jr. (class of 1876), nephew of the famous poet. The house was completed in 1900, and the gate followed in 1906. Though it's one of a limited number of Yard gates not designed by McKim, Mead & White, it does possess the same colonial feel: a veritable wrought-iron collage, fourteen feet tall at its apex and bound on both sides by stately pillars of Harvard brick. The actual swinging gates are just shy of three feet wide. It's clear in the finer details that Longfellow took the mandate to memorialize Brooks seriously: at the very top, a cross encircled by a wreath commemorates the reverend's penning of the "Bethlehem" lyrics, and just above the gate itself, an inscription honors his commitment to scripture: "Ye Shall Know the Truth and the Truth Shall Make You Free."

ABOVE: The wrought-iron decoration of the Class of 1881 Gate stands out against the white backdrop of Harvard's neoclassical Littauer Center.
PREVIOUS: Reverend Phillips Brooks's commitment to scripture is honored in an inscription on the gate. "Ye Shall Know the Truth," it says, "and the Truth Shall Make You Free."

Phillips Brooks House and its organization have certainly lived up to their namesake. Although Longfellow also shaped several buildings at the former Radcliffe College, Phillips Brooks House is by far his most significant contribution. "While largely overlooked, Longfellow's design for Phillips Brooks House is of utmost historical importance," writes Margaret Henderson Floyd in her book *Architecture after Richardson*. "It is the first instance at Harvard where archaeologically accurate quotations from extant colonial and federal buildings were incorporated in a new design. Longfellow introduced a new hierarchy that established the priority of site-specific planning and contextuality within which creativity persisted, one that would control Harvard architecture for 50 years." The nonprofit under the house's roof likewise boasts a legacy that would do Brooks proud, providing as it does an umbrella for scores of student-directed public service–oriented programs.

But the Class of 1881 Gate has long been reduced to a vestigial organ. It is open each year during the twenty-fifth reunion—mainly to accommodate guests who use Phillips Brooks House as their headquarters during reunion week. Aside from that singular event, no one in or around the house seems to remember it ever being open. The best guess, ventured by Bob Kelly, the building's operations manager, is that it was locked (and the building's main entrance moved to its south, Yard-facing side) in the early 1960s for security reasons.

That's not for a lack of careful planning on Longfellow's part. From the fine details and inscription atop the gate, all the way down to the footpath that passes beneath, his striving for harmony and continuity persisted. "I would suggest that instead of a gravel walk," he wrote to university president Charles William Eliot, in one of countless letters dissecting his plans for the house and gate, "we use stepping stones or flagging, two lines of them, with grass between. In this way we get a quaint approach to the building, as little evident as possible."

As little evident indeed. But there's hope yet: both the expansion of the Harvard Art Museums and the new plaza above the Cambridge Street underpass are drawing additional foot traffic to the north side of the Yard—enough to justify unlocking this forgotten treasure.

A Portal of Power and Delicacy

BY BLAIR KAMIN

There was no lack of creative power in Harvard's class of 1876. Among its members were the astronomer Percival Lowell, who began the effort that led to the discovery of Pluto. (His initials, PL, live on in the dwarf planet's name.) The class's ranks also included two architects who went on to establish distinguished careers: Alexander Wadsworth Longfellow Jr. and William Mitchell Kendall, who joined the firm McKim, Mead & White and designed Manhattan's stately Municipal Building. As fate would have it, the architect classmates designed side-by-side Harvard Yard gates: Longfellow, the handsome Class of 1881 Gate in front of Phillips Brooks House; Kendall, the elegantly simple gate for his own class.

Located on the Yard's north side, Kendall's Class of 1876 (Holworthy) Gate was built for $6,000, the equivalent of nearly $140,000 today. Like the brick dormitory alongside it, the gate was named for Sir Matthew Holworthy, a British benefactor who gave Harvard its largest gift of the seventeenth century.

The 1876 Gate casts its spell through architectural counterpoint. The paneled brick walls on its flanks play off against tall picket fences that curve gently backward toward its culminating wrought-iron arch. The walls' opaqueness magnifies the transparency of the fence and vice versa. The gate is simultaneously present and absent, a border that, if closed, can stop the body but not the eye.

Details are crisply handled—fine scrollwork, foliate ornament, and the palmlike petals of a crowning anthemion. Even the branches of the Yard's overhanging trees seem drawn into the composition.

The gate plays a significant urban design role, leading to a long pathway that cuts directly across the Yard to the 1857 Gate alongside Lehman Hall. The portal also frames fine outward views, including one of the thick steel roof trusses of Harvard's Science Center. Again, a telling contrast: the crudeness of the trusses underscores the delicacy of the gate's wrought iron.

The Yard-facing side of the gate's shield celebrates its dedication on Commencement Day, 1901, when, as a later class report noted, the gate was "decked with garlands gay." The shield's outward-facing side is inscribed with a nostalgic quotation from "The Ballad of the Bouillabaisse" by the nineteenth-century English novelist William Makepeace Thackeray: "In memory," it says, "of dear old times."

OVERLEAF: Solid brick walls and piers contrast with see-through wrought-iron fencing to create an interplay of opposites at the Class of 1876 Gate.

A Busy Entry
from a Quiet Donor

BY RACHEL WEHR

Class spirit transformed Harvard into the definitive gated community it is today, but Harvard's first two gates have a darker story. Two weddings and one funeral united an architect, a patron, and a wife: Harvard's holy trinity forged the university's iconic image for decades to come.

In 1885 architect Charles McKim and future US ambassador George von L. Meyer were married on the same day, in the same town, only forty-five minutes apart. They were both Harvard men, and they came as close as they could to marrying the same woman—the Appleton sisters, well-known Boston socialites Julia and Marian Alice.

Only a year later, McKim's wife, Julia, unexpectedly passed away, drawing the remaining three closer together. At Trinity Church in 1888, the architect and Marian Alice memorialized Julia with a stained-glass window. Their dearly departed could not have been far from their minds when, a year later, the triumvirate began to build an architectural legacy with the Johnston and Meyer (Class of 1879) Gates. Johnston Gate came first, and the triumphal gated arch was a tough act for Meyer to follow. When McKim ran out of money before completing Johnston Gate, Marian Alice came to his aid, donating in excess of $6,000 to finish the job, enough that McKim did not have to skimp on the gate's masterful array of ironwork.

In 1890, seemingly spurred on by his wife's interest in his alma mater's architecture (or at least by an interest in McKim's success),

Meyer offered his own gift to the college: another gate at the northern entrance to the Yard, for which he gave an unrecorded—probably very large—sum. Meyer's gate rises to the challenge posed by Johnston, but does not quite meet it. The ironwork above the gate is more open and less intricate, failing to provide a comforting sense of enclosure. The rounded brick archways, just seven feet tall, are not in keeping with the grandeur of the central passage. At Johnston, in contrast, all the parts are carefully proportioned, forming a persuasive whole.

Meyer, a member of the class of 1879, was remarkably silent on his reasons for giving the gate. His son later confessed that he had never thought to seek an explanation for the donation, and his father never supplied one. Evidence that the gift is Meyer's is only apparent in two curling *M*s hidden in the ironwork above the gate and a small shield that displays his class year. The limestone tablets that celebrate him, including one that depicts a pelican feeding her young (a Christian symbol of self-sacrifice), are worn beyond recognition. In 1944 a university archivist gently suggested to Meyer's son that a plaque might make the name of the gate more obvious. The son declined, subjecting the gate's identity to continued confusion.

ABOVE: Curving wrought-iron scrolls top the Meyer (Class of 1879) Gate, including two versions of the letter *M* that celebrate the gate's patron, Harvard alumnus George von L. Meyer. As this picture shows, the light in the gate's lantern is missing. PREVIOUS: The U-shaped entry consists of a central carriage gate flanked by urn-topped brick piers and arched foot gates. The thin spire of Harvard's Memorial Church rises in the background.

Since at least 1957, the college's student-run newspaper, the *Harvard Crimson*, has consistently and inaccurately called Meyer Gate "Thayer Gate," in reference to a nearby freshman dorm. The daily sponsored by Harvard's administration, the *Harvard Gazette*, occasionally makes the same slipup. Even some university maps call it Thayer. Glory can be bought at Harvard, but because of the continuing printed mistakes, Thayer gets it for free.

Meyer, on the other hand, fades into what Ralph Waldo Emerson once called the "longer train of ghosts" of Harvard's history. That phrase, which described a Harvard jubilee, adorns a limestone tablet on a curving brick wall that beckons students into the Yard through Meyer Gate.

Still, in some ways, function trumps fashion. When classes are in session, Meyer Gate is the most heavily trafficked of the Yard's entries, framing the main thoroughfare between the River Houses and Harvard's biggest classrooms. Viewed in this light, McKim's design for Meyer seems remarkably foresighted. The gate's flanking walls of brick help to funnel the throngs of students pushing through after classes—a narrower U-shape like the one at Johnston Gate would cause a perpetual traffic jam. Students flood through the carriage opening beneath the scrollwork, with the more courageous choosing to dart through either of the clogged brick foot gates.

McKim could not have predicted the Science Center that would rise monolithically behind the gate he designed for Meyer, nor could he have anticipated the lively plaza, designed by landscape architect Chris Reed, between the giant modern building and the Yard. The stark division between the modern plaza and the ancient gate draws the eye to Meyer's shabby disrepair. The central lantern in the iron latticework has neither a light nor panes of glass. Two colossal garbage cans sit beside the gate, unhidden and unashamed.

The story of Meyer's gate is one full of love, loss, nepotism, mortality, disrepair, and the brave new world of the Science Center plaza. George von L. Meyer and his web of relationships would forever shape this gated university.

A Nod to Women at Harvard

BY MELISSA SIMONETTI

The next time you stroll around the north end of Harvard Yard, stop and take in the diminutive Bradstreet Gate, the first gate to recognize the presence of women on campus. Bradstreet is easy to miss, not only because of its small scale, but also because its traditional looks lead you to believe it has been there forever.

In keeping with the Beaux-Arts principle of symmetry, the wrought-iron gate's archway is adorned by a balanced design featuring scrolls of varying shapes and sizes. Two working lanterns complete the traditional tableau. But while the gate looks old, it actually was built in 1995 and dedicated two years later to the first published poet of the American colonies, Anne Dudley Bradstreet. The 1997 dedication also marked the twenty-fifth anniversary of women living in the Yard's dorms. The portal's crowning arch denotes this dedication year, in contrast to the numbers on other Yard gates, which represent the year of their sponsoring class. Tablets on the flanks honor Bradstreet and the move of women into the Yard.

Designed by Boston architect Michael Teller, the gate was built to deal with the increase in foot traffic caused by Harvard's decision to relocate the freshman union to nearby Memorial Hall, the Victorian Gothic edifice built in the 1870s. If nothing else, the gate was an urban design improvement that replaced a rundown chain-link fence. Its architecture was inspired by the philosophy of contextualism: instead of creating a brazen contemporary addition to the

Yard's gates, Teller extended into the present Harvard's tradition of wrought-iron craft.

The process of making traditional architecture anew captivated Teller. In the digital age, most architects sketch their buildings on the computer, a process that is anything but tactile. In contrast, Teller reveled in making clay molds of the gate's details. They were transformed into wood pieces and finally into the ironwork we see today. Such details abound, some with an intended feminine touch. Instead of militaristic spearheads, such as those found throughout the Yard's fencing, the bottom posts of this gate are adorned by small tulips. The floral motif continues on the gate's posts, where the background for the Harvard *H* suggests a thriving flower.

OVERLEAF, LEFT: The open doors of the Bradstreet Gate reveal Harvard's Science Center plaza and the center's boldly stepped profile.
OVERLEAF, RIGHT: The wrought-iron posts of the gate display a Harvard *H* superimposed on geometric ornament.

The Yard's Only
Double Gate

BY LICIA SKY

There is a photo in the 1923 class yearbook that shows a serene but grand entrance into Harvard Yard. Two majestic street-side elms both frame and echo the ironwork portals of a magnificent gate, a recessed semicircle wide enough—at sixty-six feet—to accommodate plenty of foot traffic. That space still exists today, but it has been jettisoned and neglected.

The double gate was designed by McKim, Mead & White and erected in 1906. Alone among the twenty-five gates surrounding Harvard Yard, it was funded by two classes, 1887 and 1888. They pooled their resources to build a gate with far more presence than if either had acted alone. The gate cost more than $13,000, worth at least $300,000 today.

Originally showcasing the multihued Harvard brick and exquisite wrought-iron flourishes that are the signature of the Yard's gates, this recessed curve was as much a destination as it was a portal. A semicircle with twin foot gates, its centerpiece was a granite basin with a lion's head fountain. A fine paving material—herringbone brick—further distinguished the room-like outdoor space. So did its landscaping. There were shrubs and flowering plants along the inside of the gates. In the center, a tall commanding elm swept over the top of the arc and anchored the gates to the yard's interior landscape.

One can't help but think it must have made for a lovely gathering spot—a place where students could meet en route to church or class.

Instead, present-day passersby find only dead space and a portal in a state of serious disrepair. The gate is physically and visually overwhelmed by the well-meaning but misguided design of the modern four-story dorm, Canaday Hall, next door.

There is no longer a path leading through the shuttered footgates. All foliage and plantings along the inside of the gates have been removed, rendering the grass yard within the portal overexposed to the street and an adjoining Harvard facilities department parking lot. The grass yard is a barren plot cut through with an asphalt path—one that goes from nowhere to nowhere. It has no relationship even to the dorm it borders.

A lone streetlight stands awkwardly within the arc of the 1888 footgate. The gates' volutes and spearheads are rusted and chipped. The lion's head fountain is broken and disfigured. The semicircle, once flanked by stately elms, is now bordered by a footpath along a busy underpass. Water and dissolved limestone stains streak white along the gate's brick face. Saplings growing along the top of the arc are surely and steadily making their way through the limestone and mortar, leaving large cracks in the top of the gateway.

But even more tragic than these physical markers of decay is the opportunity that is being missed. Although Canaday Hall prevents the Classes of 1887 and 1888 Gate from being a viable passageway to Harvard Yard, the semicircle can and should be activated as a pavilion, one that reflects an important part of the history and legacy of the Yard, and the dedication of the classes that made it possible.

Basic maintenance should be addressed, beginning with the urgent task of removing the saplings. Placing shrubs and trees on the gate's Yard-facing side and along heavily trafficked Broadway would visually (and aurally) enclose the space. Seating would also help, especially if it was placed in front of the twin foot gates. By blocking the portals, it would bring a respectful finality to their closing while encouraging passersby to stop, sit, and enjoy the Yard's only double gate.

OPPOSITE: Streaks mar the brickwork and the once-proud lion's face atop the fountain of the Classes of 1887 and 1888 Gate.
PREVIOUS SPREAD: Frozen in time, the gate has two locked portals, neither of which connects with pathways leading through the Yard. Memorial Hall is in the background.

No Sizzling Design

BY BLAIR KAMIN

Many of Harvard Yard's gates are impressive works of urban art—grand portals worthy of a great university, even a royal estate. On the other end of the spectrum is the unremarkable Fire Station Gate across the street from the Georgian Revival headquarters of the Cambridge Fire Department at 491 Broadway.

When I stopped by to learn more about the gate, I talked to James Burns, the department's assistant chief. My first question wasn't about the gate, but rather about Burns's last name, which struck me as, well, comical for a fireman. I wondered: Does Burns ever get ribbed about it?

"I was going to name my children 'first, second, and third degree,'" he replied, clearly having been asked the question before. "But I knew that wouldn't go over well with my wife."

The assistant chief works in "The Big House," which is what Cambridge firefighters call their imposing but graceful three-story building. With its refined brick sheathing, richly detailed limestone trim, and eye-grabbing red cupola (the only color fit for a fire station), "The Big House" harmonizes with Harvard better than even some Harvard buildings, especially the nearby Canaday Hall, a banal brick dorm built in 1974. One wonders if the men of Engine Company 1, Ladder Company 1, and Rescue Company 1 appreciate that they work in a firehouse equipped with Palladian windows. If this firehouse lined a grassy quad, rather than sitting marooned in Broadway and

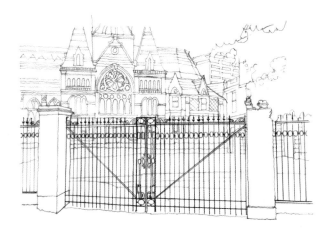

Cambridge Street's sea of asphalt, a freshman could be forgiven for walking inside in search of Math 1B.

The town-imitates-gown design was no accident. Back in the 1930s, when mighty Harvard sold Cambridge the land for the firehouse, it required that the building be dolled up in Georgian finery so it would weave seamlessly into the campus's centuries-old collegiate fabric. The archiectural firm, Sturgis Associates, complied so skillfully that, since the building's opening in 1933, many passersby on adjoining Quincy Street have not realized they were walking by a firehouse.

The Fire Station Gate, which sits just across Broadway from "The Big House" and is thought to have been installed around 1970, hardly packs as much visual punch. It's a thing of architectural prose, not poetry. In that utilitarian spirit, the gate admits garbage haulers as well as fire trucks. It's about eighteen feet wide, easily broad enough to accommodate a standard eight-foot-wide fire truck.

Except for certain details, such as the presence of diagonal support bars, the gate largely resembles the rest of the Yard's dignified enclosures. It has brick piers, as well as the obligatory decorative ovals, spear-tip finials, and studied calm. Every so often, though, a sense of urgency invades. The gate swings open to fire trucks anywhere from twenty to thirty times each year. Typically, the calls involve responding to smoke alarms triggered by burning candles, burned toast, or popcorn in the Yard's freshman dorms. If there is a fire, "Usually, we're able to get in there quick enough that we can contain it to one room," said Burns.

The fire trucks can zip through two other gates, Johnston Gate on the west and the Morgan (Class of 1877) Gate south of Widener Library. But the Fire Station Gate provides the quickest route into the Yard and, thus, the fastest way to avert the sort of disaster that struck in 1764, when the second Harvard Hall burned to the ground, and in 1956, when the tower of nearby Memorial Hall went up in flames. A conservative estimate would put the value of the Yard's buildings—among them such architectural treasures as Charles Bulfinch's University Hall and Henry Hobson Richardson's Sever Hall—in the hundreds of millions of dollars. Arguably, then, the fire station portal is the Yard's least conspicuous but most important gate.

ABOVE: The utilitarian Fire Station Gate gives fire trucks and service vehicles access
to Harvard Yard. From the inside looking out, it also affords a striking view
of Memorial Hall (left) and the Cambridge Fire Department headquarters (right).
In the background is William James Hall by Minoru Yamasaki, architect
of the World Trade Center's destroyed twin towers.

Where Michelangelo Looks Down on a Mess

BY GOKCAN DEMIRKAZIK

On one side of Quincy Street stands the imposing complex of the Harvard Art Museums, topped by a crystalline, Renzo Piano–designed steel-and-glass pavilion. But right across the street is something different: a dark, ill-kept gateway to the grandeur of Harvard Yard.

This locked portal, the Robinson Gate, once provided an entry to the basement of the Beaux-Arts Robinson Hall, which was erected in 1904 to house Harvard's architecture department. The Robinson Gate was designed by Richmond Knapp Fletcher (class of 1908) and built in 1936 as one of the four Quincy Street portals funded by the generous class of 1908. That class also sponsored the monumental Eliot Gate, the modest Emerson Gate, and the intimately scaled Loeb House Gate.

In perfect conformity with principles of symmetry, the delicate gate is flanked by a tree on either side and is aligned with Robinson Hall's central axis. The narrow metal fence posts display an admirable abundance of scrolls and volutes. The Harvard motto, however, is squeezed into the open pages of a single book (as opposed to the usual three). Apparently, even Harvard had to pare down its architectural symbolism during the hard times of the Great Depression.

The Robinson Gate's location at the Yard's northeast corner could make it a convenient entry point for pedestrians issuing forth from Divinity Avenue, the Graduate School of Design, the Center for Government and International Studies North and South, and the Sackler Museum. It actually was used this way during the renovation

and expansion of the Harvard Art Museums, when the gate was opened to provide workers a shortcut between the museums and a nearby construction trailer. When the project was completed, however, the gate was locked.

The lack of grandeur is accentuated by the accumulation of rubbish and leaves in the little pit of the basement entrance to Robinson. Limestone tablets bearing the names of such Renaissance architecture giants as Michelangelo, Palladio, and Raphael preside over this desultory tableau.

While the architect Charles McKim supposedly intended Robinson Hall to be a "background building," one meant to frame spaces rather than overwhelm them, the decoration of Robinson Hall's main facade (featuring griffins and a classically inspired tomb) puts the building in the foreground. Yet the face that Robinson Hall turns to the public along Quincy Street is in an objectionable, if not abject, state.

OVERLEAF, LEFT: The simple Robinson Gate, now locked,
once led to a sunken entrance of Robinson Hall.
OVERLEAF, RIGHT: The Harvard *H* and a single book displaying
Harvard's "Veritas" motto adorn one side of the gate.

Built by Top-Shelf Money Men

BY BLAIR KAMIN

Caviar canapés were served when Harvard's class of 1885 held its twenty-fifth anniversary dinner at Boston's Algonquin Club in 1910. So was this dollop of humor, which appeared on the menu card:

Hickory dickory dock!
The Fund climbs up the clock;
Our cash is in,
We all feel thin
Hickory dickory dock!

The class of 1885 excelled at fund-raising, almost surely because its members had plenty of funds to give. Among them was James J. Storrow of Boston, one of the twentieth century's most influential investment bankers and the third president of General Motors. Storrow left Boston a great legacy by leading the campaign to dam the Charles River, which prompted the establishment of a public park, known as the Esplanade, along the river. The riverside Storrow Drive bears his name.

Storrow's class left Harvard its own architectural legacy: a towering gate that stands as one of the major portals leading into Harvard Yard. Completed at a cost of $8,392, the equivalent of nearly $200,000 today, the Class of 1885 Gate is also known as Sever Gate because it heralds the entry into a quad headed by Henry Hobson Richardson's Sever Hall, a masterpiece of Romanesque Revival design.

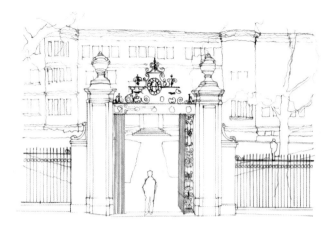

The architectural firm that designed the gate, McKim, Mead & White, also designed Sever Quad's Robinson Hall, a remarkable Beaux-Arts building that opened in the same year the gate did, 1904. For good measure, the formidable Fogg Museum, designed by Coolidge, Shepley, Bulfinch & Abbott and part of the Harvard Art Museums, sits across Quincy Street. It is an imposing context, yet the Class of 1885 Gate holds its own amid these powerful forces and even helps draw them together.

It does so by perfectly straddling the axis between Sever, built in 1880, and the Fogg, which opened its doors in 1925. Step outside one and you get a framed view of the other. And while there's an obvious neoclassical kinship between the 1885 Gate and Robinson Hall, given that McKim, Mead & White designed them both, the gate is also in harmony with Sever's exquisitely articulated mass of brownish-red brick.

Tall and refined brick piers, linked by an impressive display of wrought iron, frame the entrance. The memorable details include a wrought-iron *H* encircled by a wreath, and, atop the brick piers, limestone urns crowned with rams' heads. That flourish gave new

ABOVE: Elaborate wrought-iron decoration crowns the Class of 1885 Gate, including a large Harvard *H* and the number 85 on both sides of the letter.
OPPOSITE: Sculptured stone rams' heads adorn the urns atop the Class of 1885 Gate.
OVERLEAF: The gate frames a view of Henry Hobson Richardson's masterful Sever Hall, a classroom building.

expression to the Yard's tradition of stylized militarism, evident in the ubiquitous spear-tipped finials of its enclosing fence.

Lest anyone forget the generosity of the patrons, McKim, Mead & White included two 85s in the wrought-iron web that surmounts the portal. The class number also appears in the wrought-iron panels flanking the gate. Yet like so many other Yard gates, this one has come to take on the name of the largest building beside it, not the class that built it.

It's a lovely gate, but there's something sad about this name game—and the way it shortchanges those who once joked, "Our cash is in, We all feel thin. Hickory dickory dock!"

Handsome
but Conventional

BY ARIANA AUSTIN

Do not go where the path may lead,
go instead where there is no path and leave a trail.
— RALPH WALDO EMERSON

In 1838, when the eminent American philosopher and Harvard graduate Ralph Waldo Emerson delivered his then-infamous "Divinity School Address," his challenges to the authority of the church, as well as his emphasis on the individual and the ways nature could inform our understanding of God, were so controversial that he wasn't invited back to Harvard for thirty years.

And yet the Philosophy Department building, designed by Guy Lowell and completed in 1905, was named for Emerson himself. Its modest but attractive gate, which provided access to the building, was part of the class of 1908's gift to the university in honor of Harvard's three-hundredth anniversary. Along with the equally simple Robinson Gate and the more elaborate Eliot Gate, it was designed by Richmond Knapp Fletcher, a member of the class of 1908. Fletcher ignored Emerson's advice to break with convention and framed an existing path rather than carving a new trail. Each panel of the wrought-iron gate features a single book image from the Harvard shield emblazoned with the motto "Veritas." Below that is an *H* for Harvard along with the class number, "8." The black volutes on each side are delicate and the proportions of the gate are human scaled.

When Harvard officials named the monumental philosophy building in Emerson's honor, they chose a resolute thinker and fearless writer, one who would go on to inspire and influence the very university that spurned him. Consider that defiant spirit when you stand at the gate's threshold and observe the lovely view from Quincy Street: Emerson Hall on the left; Robinson Hall on the right; and between them, a long clear path, and the tall trees that echo on.

OVERLEAF, LEFT: The small Emerson Gate leads to a bicycle rack that echoes the visual rhythms of the gate's wrought-iron pickets. Emerson Hall is in the background.
OVERLEAF, RIGHT: A wrought-iron "8" on the gate recognizes the sponsorship of the generous class of 1908, which donated funds for four gates along Quincy Street.

A Tribute to a Towering Leader

BY ARIANA AUSTIN

One evening in June of 1891, Harvard president Charles William Eliot hosted a young W. E. B. Du Bois, the future sociologist, historian, and civil rights activist, at his home on 17 Quincy Street. It was the same year Du Bois earned his bachelor's degree from Harvard, but before he left to study in Berlin. Over a meal, and perhaps cigars, the conversation may have revolved around philosophy, race, and travel plans. It was just one of countless moments, exchanges, and interactions that took place at this landmark address.

Eliot was Harvard's president from 1869 until 1909, making the class of 1908 the last to graduate under his leadership. The class decided to honor his four decades of service to Harvard—and his many influential educational reforms—by erecting a gate in front of the president's residence. Such was their dedication to this task that, despite the Great Depression, the class managed to raise thousands of dollars for this and three other gates: Emerson, Robinson, and Loeb House, as well as twenty-five sections of fence. That was enough to complete the Yard's east side, and, with it, Eliot's great architectural vision—the enclosure of Harvard Yard.

"It was a grand job, coming right after the banking difficulties and at the bottom of the business depression," wrote class treasurer Dwight S. Brigham in 1935.

Designed by class member Richmond Knapp Fletcher of the firm Cram & Ferguson, the Eliot (Class of 1908) Gate was erected in 1936,

84

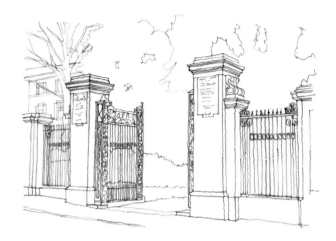

just in time for the university's Tercentenary. In addition to honoring Eliot, the gate was meant to provide an appropriately distinguished entrance to 17 Quincy Street—one worthy of the university's illustrious guests. Still, it feels modest compared to Harvard's grand portals along Massachusetts Avenue.

The gate is framed by two tall brick piers, each featuring a prominent stone tablet. The inscription on the left pier informs passersby that the class of 1908 sponsored the gate in honor of Eliot. The other tablet contains a passage selected by former Radcliffe College president LeBaron Russell Briggs and a member of the class of 1908, the American maritime historian Samuel Eliot Morison: "He opened paths

OVERLEAF, LEFT: A tribute to the namesake of the Eliot (Class of 1908) Gate accents one of the gate's piers.
OVERLEAF, RIGHT: The gate, named for Harvard's longest-serving president, Charles William Eliot, creates a simple entrance to Harvard Yard from Quincy Street. To the right of the gate is Emerson Hall.

IN MEMORY
OF
CHARLES
WILLIAM
ELIOT
1834 - 1926

GIVEN BY
THE CLASS OF 1908

ABOVE: The gate's wrought-iron decoration recognizes the sponsorship of the class of 1908. Below that tribute, a pilgrim's hat offers a whimsical nod to President Eliot's Puritan ancestors.

for our childrens [*sic*] feet to follow / Something of him will be a part of us for ever." There is something simple and true about these words.

At the dedication of the gate, John Richardson (class of 1908) said of Eliot: "He found that truth was eternal and yet each day must be sought anew. As president, his constant search for truth made him a true liberal, a true progressive, a pioneer."

Eliot's many pioneering educational reforms included advocating for a "spontaneous diversity of choice" for undergraduate education, which led to the modern elective system, and standardized testing for entry into Harvard. During his tenure, he oversaw the addition of Radcliffe College and education for women, as well as the establishment of programs in business administration and landscape architecture. Each of these reforms would ultimately spread from Harvard to universities across the nation.

Thus, the "something of him" is very much present in today's Harvard, from the entrance exams that secure admission to the classes students choose to take once here. There is also "something of him" far richer: the reconciling of American privilege and responsibility.

The famous quotes from the more elaborate Dexter Gate—"Enter to Grow in Wisdom" and "Depart to Serve Better Thy Country and Thy

Kind"—were penned by Eliot himself. Like so many words that come to us from the past, "Thy Kind" must be contextualized by the era and made relevant today. "I cannot imagine greater diversity than there is in Harvard College. It is not superficial; it is deep; it is shown in the variety of races, religious households from richest to poorest and in the mental gifts and ambitions," Eliot said in a 1911 address.

Despite his liberal ideals, Eliot's comments often reflected the attitudes of the day. "Experience does not show that blending [of races] or amalgam is advantageous. It produces an inferior breed," he said in the 1911 speech. Still, Eliot made no effort to limit the enrollment of specific groups of students, unlike his successor, A. Lawrence Lowell, who attempted to cap the number of Jewish students admitted to the college. Eliot recommended Du Bois for a scholarship at the University of Berlin, though his letter bluntly stated that "Du Bois would be considered a very promising student if he were white." Du Bois received the scholarship, and the two remained in correspondence for years to come. Ultimately, Du Bois would return to pursue higher studies, becoming in 1895 the first African American to receive a PhD from Harvard.

Today the former president's house beyond his gate is the headquarters of two governing boards: the Overseers and the Corporation. Again, the gate is an entryway for people in powerful positions who decide the future of the university. This particular path invites a calm, thoughtful meditation. We need only to pass through momentarily to be reminded of our access, privilege, and responsibility.

Where Less Is More

BY LICIA SKY

A gate doesn't have to be big to be beautiful. That's the lesson of the small, elegant gate that leads to Loeb House, once the home of Harvard presidents and now the meeting place of the university's Board of Overseers. The house is surprisingly intimate, anything but intimidating. So is the gate leading to it.

Loeb House was constructed in 1912, located at 17 Quincy Street among Harvard's grand halls, libraries, and dorms. It was donated by A. Lawrence Lowell (class of 1877), then president of Harvard, and designed by his cousin Guy Lowell (class of 1892). The house's gate was erected in 1936 as a gift of the class of 1908. Architect Lowell rendered in residential dimensions the same Harvard brick, Flemish bond, wrought-iron spears, floral details, and connecting circles of the other gates that enclose the Yard. Yet the gate doesn't overwhelm you, as the Yard's biggest gates do.

The gate is low enough for a person to easily touch the top of its opening. The opening itself is just wide enough for one person at a time to pass through. The walkway leading up to the house allows two people to comfortably approach the front door, standing side by side. The gate even sets limits in a gentle way. One would not mistake its choreographed pathway for a shortcut to surrounding lecture halls or the Lamont Library.

At first, the setting of the president's house was idyllic. A 1956 photo shows a Currier & Ives–like scene of a three-story home, at

once dignified and understated. In the photo, the symmetrical lines of the Georgian Revival home are framed by a curved drive and snow-covered trees. But in 1971 the university's newly appointed president, Derek Bok, chose to live instead in a stately colonial-era home, known as Elmwood, off Brattle Street.

The growth of the university and the need for new buildings to serve the school made for an inevitable encroachment on the private space surrounding the president's house. The Houghton Library for rare books opened in 1942, closing off the house's backyard. Lamont Library was completed in 1949, blocking both the Yard's south lawn and the house's access and view of the lovely 1880 Bacon Gate. The building of the underground Pusey Library and the campus unrest of the Vietnam War era apparently were the final factors precipitating Bok's decision to forgo living at Loeb House. According to a 2001 *Harvard Gazette* story, the library's construction "created a large hole in the residence's backyard, and, more importantly, student protests at the house had led to serious security concerns for Bok and his young family."

Loeb House's upper floors now hold the offices of the university's governing boards. The first floor includes a banquet hall and ballroom available for rent. The basement is home to a consortium of community groups. In 1995 the house was named to honor longtime Harvard donors John Langeloth Loeb and Frances Lehman Loeb. Its gate provides a fitting introduction, as gentle and gemlike as the house it heralds.

OPPOSITE, TOP: The intimate Loeb House Gate is well suited
to the character of the house to which it leads.
OPPOSITE, BOTTOM: Delicate wrought-iron numerals and details lend
a human scale to the gate and recognize its sponsoring class.

The Ultimate Vanishing Act

BY KATHY RAN

The 17 Quincy Drive Gate is an unfortunate member of Harvard Yard's enclosure. Its purpose as a driveway entrance was stripped away years ago, and members of the university do not toss the poor, neglected thing a second glance as they hobble along the narrow cobbled sidewalk. Most will not even remember it as a portal into the Yard.

The gate, which was erected around 1949, was designed by an unknown architect in the same style as the renowned McKim, Mead & White gates that encircle the Yard. It served as the driveway entrance to the residence of the university's president until the early 1970s when President Derek Bok chose to move to a more secluded home off Brattle Street. Despite its fine brick piers and simple but beautiful wrought-iron work, the 17 Quincy Drive Gate was locked permanently with the 1972 installation of Henry Moore's *Large Four Piece Reclining Figure* in Lamont Yard. It essentially became a fence for a sculpture garden, vanishing into the structure to which it once provided an opening.

Still, there is something to be said for the fence's sense of transparency. Looking through the gate from Quincy Street, one can see Lamont Library, a modern Bauhaus-like undergraduate center for homework, research, writing, cramming, afternoon napping, and exam-time sleeping. Lamont is juxtaposed with Houghton Library, Harvard's Georgian Revival–styled treasure trove. Unity is maintained in these disparate buildings by the use of the characteristic Harvard brick and white limestone trim.

In the swath of grass behind the gate is a more startling image: Henry Moore's mind-bending sculpture. Its surrealism-invoking design calls into question its role in this colonial-flavored sanctuary. A connection to its surroundings is revealed when the visitor walks into the Yard and looks across the street toward the Carpenter Center for the Visual Arts. The center appears as a concrete playground designed by Le Corbusier, complete with a levitating ramp that runs through the facade.

The forgotten status of the gate is ultimately not a loss for the Harvard community, as it still signals the restrained atmosphere that prevails in the Yard. "I have never thought of Harvard's gates in terms of security," said Melissa Sieffer, class of 2014. "It's more about the fact that you know you have entered into quiet land." Together, the gate and its flanking fences inform passersby that inside is a contemplative ambience to be respected—and to save the ruckus for the architectural statements that run amok beyond the Yard.

OVERLEAF: The 17 Quincy Drive Gate originally served as a driveway entrance for the house of Harvard's president. Locked since 1972, when Henry Moore's *Large Four Piece Reclining Figure* was installed, the gate now blends inconspicuously into the fence around Harvard Yard.

The Ghost That Still Haunts

BY BLAIR KAMIN

Lamont Library's two gates would hardly be worth a tweet if they weren't haunted by a ghost: the ghost of the long-gone Dudley Memorial Gate, which materialized along Quincy Street nearly a century ago, complete with a jaunty clock tower and an error chiseled in stone.

The gate lasted just thirty-two years until 1947, when it was torn down to make way for Lamont, the Yard's first modernist building, and the simple brick piers that lead to its front entrance and rear delivery zone. Amid the regal artistry and rigid symmetry of McKim, Mead & White's Harvard gates, Dudley was an oddball—quirky and asymmetrical, more interesting than good. Appropriately, a rich aunt paid for this, the crazy old uncle of the Yard's gates.

The patron, Caroline Stokes, bequeathed the then-princely sum of $25,000, the equivalent of more than $588,000 today, to her nephew, New York architect I. N. Phelps Stokes. She stipulated that he use the money to build a memorial at Harvard to her ancestor, Thomas Dudley (1576–1653). Dudley had sailed on the *Arabella* with the Puritans, helped found Harvard, and governed the Massachusetts Bay Colony. Stokes's initial plan called only for a clock tower to honor the great man. But as the *Boston Evening Transcript* reported when it unveiled the design in 1914, Harvard president A. Lawrence Lowell suggested that the tower be made part of a large gateway. The finished gate, which opened in 1915 and was easily the most expensive of

the Yard's gates, lent credence to the adage that a camel is a racehorse designed by committee.

Brick piers of varying height and girth flanked a recessed central passageway crowned by ornate wrought iron. The taller pier, thirty-six feet high, sported a domed clock tower with gilded hands. (The gilt was added after Harvard building officials complained it was difficult to see the hands.) Such was "Harvard time," circa 1915. Curving brick walls with arched foot gates led to elaborate piers along the sidewalk.

While the design failed to match the eloquent standard set by McKim, Mead & White at the Johnston Gate, it still retained the palette of brick, stone, and wrought iron used in earlier gates; it also framed a view of the Hallowell Gate across Quincy Street. Stokes called the style "Colonial"; historians dubbed it "Tudor." It was, if nothing else, eclectic—and error-ridden, most notably on the Yard-facing side of the clock tower, where a questionable claim appeared beneath a bas-relief sculpture of the gate's namesake. It read, "First Governor of Massachusetts."

"Harvard Tower Has Graven Error," a *New York Tribune* headline trumpeted on June 15, 1915.

As Harvard professor Albert B. Hart pointed out, the distinction of being the state's first leader belonged to John Winthrop, not Dudley. Shaken, Stokes and his colleagues at the architectural firm of Howells & Stokes sent an apologetic letter and telegram to Harvard, the latter requesting that the error be "neatly covered." Harvard, in turn, pasted limestone-colored paper over the flub. Ever the unflappable Boston Brahmin, Lowell offered no hint that the mistake bothered him.

"Slips will occur," he wrote to Stokes on June 23, 1915. "That can be changed in due time. The bas-relief itself seems to me admirable. Late in the afternoon the old Puritan positively winks at you."

More than sixty-five years after its demolition, regret persists over the fate of the Dudley Memorial Gate, a sentiment voiced in a 2005 *Harvard Gazette* story that, perhaps too charitably, likened the lost gate to "other vanished architectural wonders like the Colossus of Rhodes or Pennsylvania Station."

All that's left of the gate are the curving stone benches that adorned its Yard-side flanks. They can be found in the Dudley Garden, a serene and secluded outdoor space behind Lamont that opened in 1949 and was handsomely redesigned by the landscape architect Michael Van Valkenburgh to mark the fiftieth anniversary of the library's completion.

So much for the Dudley Memorial Gate's expensive, outside-the-box flamboyance.

PREVIOUS: With its off-center clock tower, the Dudley Memorial Gate was a striking presence along Quincy Street, departing from the symmetry of the Harvard Yard gates shaped by McKim, Mead & White.
OPPOSITE, TOP: The utilitarian Lamont Library service gate looks onto a blank brick wall and garbage bins.
OPPOSITE, BOTTOM: The simple brick and limestone piers of the Lamont Library Gate frame a view of the library, the first modernist addition to Harvard Yard.

A Singular Portal
Breathes with Life

BY GOKCAN DEMIRKAZIK

The side of Harvard that faces the city of Boston—the first glimpse one catches of fair Harvard when arriving from Massachusetts Avenue—is an imposing brick wall with a powerfully composed white limestone gate dominating its center. Both the gate and the wall are exceptions to the rest of the McKim, Mead & White–designed brick and wrought-iron enclosures of Harvard Yard, even though Charles McKim himself designed them. And the Bacon (Class of 1880) Gate is even more of an exception because it is the only gate that breathes.

The Bacon Gate breathes quietly and slowly. Its inhalations and exhalations are deep and season-long: In the winter its forlorn bulk projects forward, with the hibernating ivies wrapped around its sharp features. In the spring the gate almost disappears under the ferocious invasion of foliage. Ivies cover the classical details—triglyphs, metopes, dentils—beneath Harvard's trademark "Veritas" shield. What can be glimpsed of the gate's triangular pediment is an outline with occasional patches of limestone glinting in the sun.

The gate's changing faces hint at its original conception as a primary entrance to the Yard. Built in 1902 for a stunning sum of $16,173, or roughly $375,000 today, the Bacon Gate reflected McKim's ambitions to sculpt the Harvard landscape according to the City Beautiful aesthetic of axial organization and monumental symmetry. Part of his plan was to convert humble DeWolfe Street into a tree-lined boulevard connecting the Charles River to a major portal into the Yard. Although

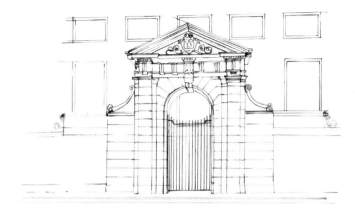

these plans failed to materialize, the Bacon Gate remained—a vestige of McKim's grand project.

From one end of narrow and winding DeWolfe, the Bacon Gate stands out, and not only because it is the Yard's only all-limestone gate. Its Doric features bestow the gate with a strong sense of masculinity not found in the delicate details of other Yard entries. The gate's rusticated piers accentuate its presence, while the sheer thickness of its deep-set archway conjures an image of toughness.

The transitions from the brick retaining walls to the limestone gate are rendered masterfully smooth, thanks to the walls' limestone trim and balustrades. The walls themselves bow out in a fortresslike fashion, making the gate their centerpiece—quite unlike McKim's recessed-curve gates found elsewhere around the Yard.

Capped on both ends by monumental urns, each with a sculpted pair of lions' heads, the retaining walls feature tablets inscribed with the names of the benefactor, Robert Bacon, and his longtime friend, former US president Theodore Roosevelt. Born in the Boston neighborhood of Jamaica Plain, Bacon was a member of the class of 1880 and later became a partner of the celebrated financier J. P. Morgan.

Friends in college, Bacon and Roosevelt were linked throughout their lives. In 1905, as part of Roosevelt's administration, Bacon became the assistant secretary of state. When Secretary of State Elihu Root retired in 1909, Bacon assumed the vacant position. During the following three years, he would serve as the US ambassador to France. The names of Bacon and Roosevelt, 1880 class secretary John Woodbury has asserted, "must always be linked together."

Built in 1949 and resembling a giant brick, the Lamont Library serves as an effective backdrop for the gate. It allows the white gate to "pop" while at the same time creating an underlying harmony with the portal through its off-white limestone window trim. Yet something is amiss in this serene tableau: ever since unspecified "illicit activity" took place behind the gate during the era of student unrest in the late 1960s, the gate has been locked, rendering it a mere relic.

Peering through the iron wings of the gate, the passerby encounters a brick wall marked by a stone tablet inscribed with "Class of 1880." On either side of the wall are steps leading to the Dudley Garden, a hidden jewel of a terrace.

The view through the wings reveals another exceptional aspect of the Bacon Gate: it was the Yard's only gate that involved an ascent from street level to higher ground. It was, in other words, a processional gate, one that demanded a proper etiquette. Yet now, with the Bacon Gate locked, the once-dynamic relationship between the gate and its landscape has been severely sapped.

To be sure, the Dudley Garden compensates. Redesigned by Michael Van Valkenburgh and finished in 1999 to mark the fiftieth anniversary of the Lamont Library, it is accessible from April to October via a smaller gate wedged between one end of Wigglesworth Hall and the closed Pusey Library entrance.

OPPOSITE: The Bacon (Class of 1880) Gate, Harvard Yard's
only all-limestone portal, is wrapped in ivy vines.
Lamont Library is in the background.

Even to the unknowing eye, the path to the garden evinces that a wonderland lies ahead, with lines winding slightly uphill, accompanied by what looks like a giant concrete mushroom. The garden itself, due to its elevation from Massachusetts Avenue and its seclusion from the Yard, does not belong to either world. It is uncontrived and beautifully simple, with two long C-shaped stone benches (remnants of the demolished Dudley Memorial Gate) and a bluestone sundial in the middle. (The sundial is one of the few in the world that tell daylight saving time.)

Sandwiched between Lamont Library's brick block and the high brick walls of the Bacon Gate, the Dudley Garden is a shelter with more than enough peace as well as sufficient room for visitors to breathe and contemplate the legacy of Bacon through his namesake portal. As Bishop Charles Henry Brent said of Bacon at his funeral, "His life is embedded in the life of the country and the world of men. He lives a hero with the heroes." He really lives on at Harvard, not just with his name attributed to a gate, but especially through the state of his gate—alive and breathing.

OPPOSITE: A limestone plaque adorns the bowing retaining wall of the Bacon Gate, honoring the gate's chief benefactor, Robert Bacon, a partner of financier J. P. Morgan and ambassador to France.

As Notable for Its Words as Its Form

BY BECCA MAZUR

With the possible exception of Harvard's motto, "Veritas," the university's most famous quote is inscribed above the entrance to Dexter (Class of 1890) Gate. Widely cited in commencement speeches and *Harvard Crimson* editorials, and captured as well in tourist photos, the phrase "Enter to Grow in Wisdom" is even immortalized in commemorative handmade bookends sold online. But the quote might have read quite differently if earlier versions considered by Josephine Dexter, the mother of the gate's namesake, had been used.

As archival documents reveal, Dexter discussed with Harvard president Charles William Eliot the possibility that the phrase read "Enter Daily to Grow in Wisdom." The two also considered that the inscription on the reverse side of the gate be "Depart to Serve Better Thy Country and Mankind," rather than "Thy Kind." Though neither is vastly different, they would have subtly elicited other interpretations, differently situating the gate in the minds of students and tourists alike. "Enter Daily to Grow in Wisdom" sounds prescriptive and instructional rather than inspiring and inviting.

The alternative for the interior inscription might have been advisable. As Harvard professor John Stilgoe pointed out in a 2011 video about Harvard Yard, "Depart to Serve Better Thy Country and Thy Kind" prompts the question: Who exactly is included in one's kind—all mankind or just other educated people? Harvard's history of discrimination seems to validate concerns that though this statement sounds

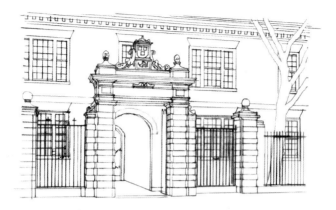

noble, it is actually an expression of elitism. "Mankind" has a much clearer, obviously inclusive, and benevolent meaning. There were still other options discussed for this inscription that thankfully are long forgotten, including the phrases "useful to thy country" or, worse, "serviceable to thy brothers."

Apart from the memorable quote, Dexter Gate, also known as the Class of 1890 Gate, is a beautiful structure in its own right. It cost almost $4,200, which is worth about $100,000 today. In many ways, it resembles its sister—the Class of 1889 Gate, which sits to the west on Massachusetts Avenue. The two are "of practically the same motive of design," wrote Walter Dana Swan in the *Architectural Review* in 1901, the year both gates were completed. The siblings feature an eye-catching pattern of alternating stripes of smooth limestone and rough brick. Unique among the Yard's gates, the pattern evokes a rustic gate design of the Renaissance architect Sebastiano Serlio. It was an appropriate choice, because Serlio's gate was designed as the entrance

OVERLEAF: The Dexter (Class of 1890) Gate, famous for its "Enter to Grow in Wisdom" quotation, belongs to a row of prominent Harvard gates along Massachusetts Avenue. Wigglesworth Hall is in the background.

ABOVE: The oft-cited quotation "Enter to Grow in Wisdom" was selected by Harvard president Charles William Eliot.

to a villa in a park. Similarly, at the beginning of the twentieth century, the scene inside the Yard was practically a pastoral expanse, scattered with trees.

The wrought-iron work of these portals is far less ornate than that of other Yard gates, yet the delicate floral designs and spear motifs use the same visual vocabulary as the rest of Harvard's fencing. Likewise, the brick pattern and use of limestone fit comfortably with other Harvard gates and buildings.

While architectural firm McKim, Mead & White originally planned the Dexter Gate and the Class of 1889 Gate to be identical, the design for Dexter was altered to allow space for the inscriptions at the request of Josephine Dexter. Her son, Samuel Dexter (class of 1890), died in 1894, two days after coming down with cerebrospinal meningitis.

Dexter had been president of his class, and a *Crimson* obituary described him as "one of the most promising of the recent graduates of Harvard. He was universally admired and respected." In college he'd been a member of what another obituary deemed "all the best societies," including the Hasty Pudding, the A.D. Club, and the Institute of 1770 (a social club since absorbed by the Hasty Pudding), as well as the varsity football team.

In 1931 Dexter Gate's surroundings were dramatically altered with the construction of Wigglesworth Hall. The building's brick facade replaced a grassy, bucolic expanse as the backdrop of Dexter Gate. Many of the Yard's other gates were removed or permanently locked when buildings were built behind them. Wigglesworth Hall, though, was designed to permit the continued usage of both the Dexter and the Class of 1889 Gates.

Still, the presence of Wigglesworth inexorably alters the aura of Dexter Gate. Whereas once the entrance stood alone, taller than everything in its proximity except trees, the building now overshadows it. The windows and slightly different-colored brick distract from the gate, and passing through the arched tunnel under Wigglesworth seems a more memorable experience than passing through the gate. Though flocks of tourists stop to photograph the "Enter to Grow in Wisdom" inscription, the ceiling of the tunnel decreases the likelihood that their gaze will happen upon "Depart to Serve Better Thy Country and Thy Kind."

Just as the landscape around the gate has grown more complex and distracting, the simple values of wisdom and service that President Eliot and Josephine Dexter wanted to convey are not always straightforward goals. Dexter Gate nonetheless stands as both a beautiful portal and an inspirational symbol of the most noble of aims to which this or any university could aspire.

Too Big for Its Own Good?

BY MELISSA SIMONETTI

It's towering and extravagant, reflecting the larger-than-life Edwin D. Morgan. Soaring about 30 feet above Massachusetts Avenue and 240 feet wide, the Morgan Gate (otherwise known as the Class of 1877 Gate), is Harvard Yard's tallest and boldest portal. But at times, it's too big for its own good.

The gate's grandeur may come as a puzzle, given that it's hemmed in by storefronts across Massachusetts Avenue. The gate is a product of the City Beautiful movement, an urban planning initiative that introduced monuments and magnificence to America's cities during the late nineteenth and early twentieth centuries. Large-scale civic projects, like the extension of the National Mall between the Washington Monument and Lincoln Memorial, transformed city centers nationwide. City Beautiful advocates, among them Charles McKim of McKim, Mead & White, believed that orderly and harmonious cityscapes could produce a better quality of life.

Reflecting these ideals, McKim, Mead & White anticipated that Morgan Gate would eventually be approached by a grand axis, a kind of Champs-Élysées, linking the Charles River to the Yard. The architects also foresaw, and correctly so, that the gate would mark an approach to a new monumental library that would replace the undersized and outdated Gothic Revival Gore Hall. The Cambridge version of the Champs-Élysées never materialized. But the colossal Widener Library

went up in 1915, and the Morgan Gate followed due to the generosity of its swashbuckling patron.

A relative of financier J. P. Morgan, Edwin D. Morgan lived a storied life as a collector of yachts. He was a former commodore of the New York Yacht Club and the managing owner of the yacht *Columbia*, which won the America's Cup in 1899 and 1901. A report that described the winners of the Cup said there was "no more simple, unassuming man to be found either on or off the yacht." He was, by far, the largest contributor to the gate, which cost nearly $13,000, the equivalent of almost $300,000 today.

Big enough to be one of Morgan's yachts, the Morgan Gate wasn't built until the class of 1877 looked forward to its twenty-fifth reunion in 1902. The class committee proposed the gate as other Harvard classes were building gates of their own. But this gate, in keeping with the outsized personality of its donor, sought to upstage Johnston Gate and become the Yard's most important portal.

OVERLEAF: The towering Morgan Gate joins with dormitories such as Wigglesworth Hall to form a harmonious perimeter around Harvard Yard. The Widener Library is in the background.

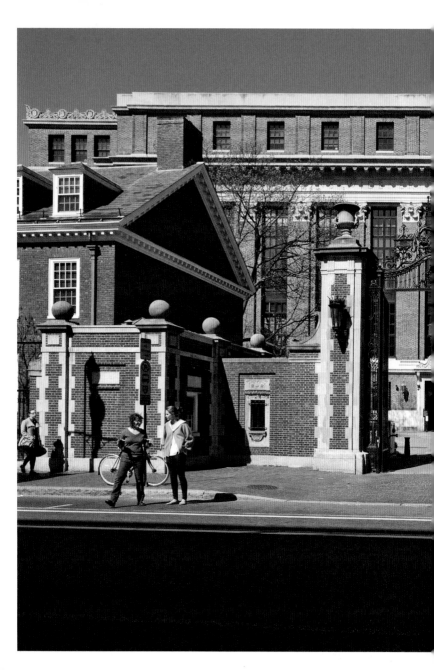

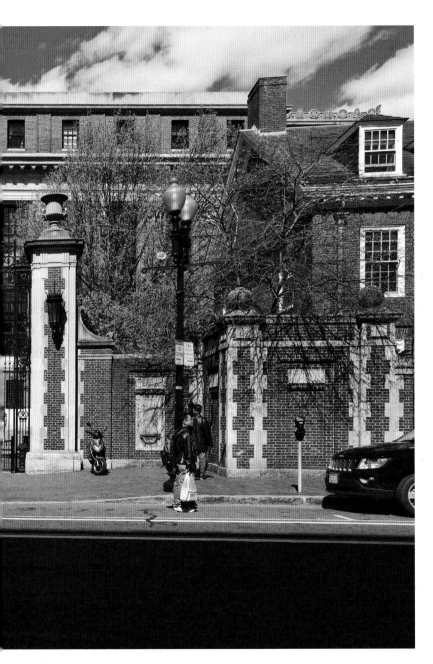

McKim's design produced a strongly vertical passageway, one framed by brick and limestone piers that drew inspiration from French Renaissance models rather than the humble Georgian buildings that inspired the Johnston Gate. Projecting pavilions were situated on the flanks in the same refined French manner—one even still contains the Harvard Yard security office. Members of the class of 1877 believed that the gate would become the most heavily used.

But it never happened. Nor did the grand approach. Lacking the distant view envisioned by the architects, Morgan's portal can seem overwhelming.

Look closely, though, and there's beauty to behold. The gate isn't just big; it's full of drop-dead delicacy, most notably in its crowning array of lacy wrought iron. On display is everything from a wreath that surrounds the numerals of the class year to foliage that springs from classical urns. Even the flanking pavilions are adorned with such visual grace notes as a handsome little grate that opens a view into the Yard. These details successfully leaven the ever-present Morgan largeness.

What can be done to improve the area around this elegant but imposing McKim design? Add a bench or two in front of Widener. Provide a place—a welcoming place—for visitors to sit and admire the view. That's all it would take to enhance Morgan's remarkable, over-sized addition to Harvard Yard.

Overshadowed by
Its Near Twin

BY BECCA MAZUR

The sibling rivalry between the Class of 1889 Gate and the class of 1890's Dexter Gate is a quite unfair competition. Dexter Gate has its own name and its iconic inscription; in comparison, the 1889 Gate is just another pretty, unmemorable class gate.

It would have been tough to top "Enter to Grow in Wisdom," but architectural firm McKim, Mead & White did include a panel intended for an inscription near the top of the gate, right below the Harvard shield. In a description of the gate sent to the class secretary, the architects wrote, "We call the attention of the class to the fact that the similarly situated panel in the gate for the class of 1890 is provided with an inscription." The secretary passed on the message to the rest of the class but they never seized the opportunity.

McKim, Mead & White originally planned the 1889 Gate and Dexter Gate, both facing Massachusetts Avenue and framing the 1877 Gate behind Widener Library, as identical twins. The design of Dexter was slightly altered, but the two gates are still quite similar. Both are distinguished from the Yard's other portals by the stripes of brick and limestone on the columns. On the 1889 Gate, the stripes continue across the flat arch and even adorn its underside.

Unlike its luckier sister, the Class of 1889 Gate was raised without a mother's love. While the Dexter Gate was funded by Josephine Dexter, the mother of the gate's namesake, the members of the class of 1889 had to raise the full cost of the gate—$5,074, equal to about $118,000

today—from among their 317 members. The endeavor was underwritten by some of the class's wealthiest members living in New York and Boston, including J. P. Morgan Jr.

Oliver Prescott was in charge of securing contributions, and in the spring of 1901 he sent a form letter to his former classmates asking for donations. He received responses ranging from $200 to $2 (the latter paid in two installments). Eventually, the fund-raising efforts were successful. The gate was dedicated at Commencement in 1902.

In 1931 Wigglesworth Hall was constructed behind the gate. The dorm was built with an archway so the gate would remain usable, but the gate's countenance was drastically altered. Always overshadowed by the Dexter Gate's fame, the 1889 Gate was now literally in the shadow of the building behind it.

OVERLEAF: The Class of 1889 Gate is striped like its sister portal, the Dexter (Class of 1890) Gate, but lacks an inscription to match "Enter to Grow in Wisdom."

Inspired by a Pig Roast

BY KATHY RAN

An odd entity greets individuals who walk through Harvard's McKean (Porcellian Club) Gate. A pig's head, carved in white limestone, sits under the ubiquitous "Veritas" emblem, leering at passersby from its lofty perch. It rests in silence and stares across the street to its mirror, another porker carved into the keystone atop an austere black door: the entrance to the secretive Porcellian Club at 1324 Massachusetts Avenue.

The pig, the idiosyncratic mascot of the ancient club, is no Harvard emblem. It comes from the long-standing history of an organization shrouded in mystery, because its members habitually abstain from commenting on their private affairs.

Colloquially known as the "P.C.," the club got its start in 1791 when Harvard student Joseph McKean chose to present a whole roast pig to the Argonauts, a student organization. This led to the name of the "Pig Club," which was then replaced by a more elegant name derived from the Latin translation, *porcus*. McKean established the philosophy of the group and served as both its secretary and grand marshal.

Since then, the mascot has not advanced much in status from the dinner table. In a 1991 leaflet describing the club's induction process, we learn that on initiation night, "They ride a pig up the stairs. This is probably quite unpleasant for the pig, but most members find it quite stimulating. Nevertheless, the pig gets his fun when he gets to ride the new initiates on the way back down." However, the savage

pig shenanigans associated with the gate are not enough to depreciate its architectural beauty. Built in honor of McKean and designed by McKim, Mead & White, it cost $6,726, at least $155,000 in today's dollars.

Unlike other Yard gates, with their delicate webs of wrought iron, this portal is a brick heavyweight. A coffered ceiling tops its deep, U-shaped archway. The gate's flanking wings exhibit airy, wrought-iron fences in which the letters *PC* are adeptly inscribed. Paneled brick walls with tributes to the founder complete the gate's small plaza along Massachusetts Avenue.

OVERLEAF, LEFT: Symbolizing the gate's donor—the Porcellian Club, one of Harvard's social, or "final," clubs—a white limestone pig adorns the keystone of the McKean (Porcellian Club) Gate. The club got its start in 1791 when Harvard student Joseph McKean fed a student organization with a whole roast pig.
OVERLEAF, LEFT: A brick heavyweight amid Harvard Yard's delicate portals of wrought iron, the McKean Gate is distinguished by its coffered, deeply recessed arch.

In addition to achieving status as an accomplished piece of architecture, the McKean Gate is skillfully woven into the fabric of its urban setting. It sits near the entrance to Harvard Square's subway stop and serves as a benched waiting area for the number 1 bus to Dudley Station.

To some the gate is overwhelmed by neighboring Wigglesworth Hall, which imitates the portal's classical features but also crowds it. "Now if you're asking about a gate covered in candy cane carvings, I'd know exactly what you're talking about, but to the untrained eye, the [McKean] gate is just a part of the enclosure," said George Fu (class of 2013), who lived in Wigglesworth during his freshman year. In fact, not even Harvard's own shuttle service addresses the gate by its proper name—it's commonly called "Boylston Gate," after nearby Boylston Hall.

The McKean Gate is a burdened member of the Yard border, struggling to make its presence separate from Wigglesworth Hall. However, it is hard to say that this gate suffers from conformity any more than its brethren do. We can still give it credit for its long-standing dedication to serving as a passageway that combines utility with eccentric beauty.

OPPOSITE: Wrought-iron scrolls, surrounded by a circle, spell out the Porcellian Club's initials in the fencing that flanks the McKean Gate.

A Tribute to Bonds
Not Broken by Civil War

BY BLAIR KAMIN

The handsome, intimately scaled Class of 1857 Gate quietly celebrates bonds of friendship—in particular, the ties between Harvard class-mates, from the North and South, which remained unbroken in spite of the Civil War's controversy and carnage.

While the debate over slavery divided the nation, it did not split this class, at least not permanently, even though the war took the lives of at least four of its members. Among them: Henry Longer De Saulles, a "Crimson Confederate" lieutenant, and Howard Dwight, a Union captain. The two were killed in separate Louisiana battles, exactly one month apart, in the spring of 1863. The class "became so uni-fied in later years that, despite fighting the Civil War, they decided to donate money to projects such as the Class of 1857 Gate," said Matthew Chuchul, a Harvard student, in a 2011 video about the friendships between Harvard men on both sides of the fight. He said that of 1857's eighty or so members, ten were Southerners, a typical proportion at Harvard in those days.

In the years after the war, the class of 1857 donated nearly $2,000 for a large stained-glass window in the Victorian Gothic Memorial Hall, which opened in 1874. The window, heavy with Civil War overtones, appropriately illustrated the characters of scholars-turned-soldiers who died from wounds suffered in battle.

For its Harvard Yard gate, the class gave more than $5,500, the equivalent of at least $128,000 today. It was the only Civil War–era

class—and the earliest of all the classes—to sponsor a gate. Its members donated even though they would have been about sixty-five years old, well beyond the average life expectancy for an American male (forty-six), when the gate opened in 1901. Perhaps they sought a measure of immortality. If so, they did it together, not as individuals.

As contemporary observers noted, McKim, Mead & White's design was adroitly tailored to its setting. The portal rose near Dane Hall, a horizontally massed Greek Revival structure that was home to the Harvard Law School until it was destroyed by fire in 1918. The gate "is built with proportions which suggest [Dane Hall], being long and low," applauded Walter Dana Swan in a 1901 *Architectural Review* assessment.

The gate's details were equally well handled. Three low arches punctured its brick wall, with two elegant lanterns framing a slightly

OVERLEAF: Located at the southwest corner of Harvard Yard, the three-arched Class of 1857 Gate was built by Harvard alumni who were divided by the Civil War yet united by college ties.

wider central arch. The flanking openings, low and narrow, were perfectly scaled to the people passing through them. The gate was a wall but a porous wall, one that encouraged pedestrians to move freely between the quotidian and contemplative environments of Harvard Square and Harvard Yard. Atop its richly detailed limestone cornice rose four urns, each adorned in delicate, foliate ornament that suggested the Yard's parklike setting.

The gate's small scale also sympathetically addressed nearby Wadsworth House, the yellow, early eighteenth-century home that once housed Harvard presidents. This harmonious relationship became even more important in the 1920s, when Harvard moved the gate eastward to make way for Lehman Hall and Straus Hall. At that point, the gate was practically hooked to the side of the colonial relic.

Today the portal serves as an attractive, heavily trafficked link between the Yard and Harvard Square. At lunchtime professors clutching satchels and students in search of a break from classroom rigors troop through the three arches on their way to Harvard's Holyoke Center and other points across Massachusetts Avenue. After lunch the flow reverses.

Above the heads of the busy big thinkers, semicircular limestone tablets fill the gate's two side arches and offer Latin words drawn from one of Horace's odes. To read them through the eyes of the class that lived through the horrors of the Civil War is to recognize them as heartfelt contemporary messages, not arid pronouncements from long ago. The inscriptions, which were added to the gate, along with the class number, in 1909, have been translated: "Thrice happy and more are they whom an unbroken band unites, and whom no sundering of love by wretched quarrels shall separate before life's dying day."

OPPOSITE: Semicircular limestone insets fill the two side arches of the Class of 1857 Gate. The Latin inscriptions celebrate bonds of friendship that cannot be split, even by harsh quarrels, a subtle reference to the Civil War.

FELICES
TER·ET·AMPLIVS
QVOS·INRVPTA·TENET
COPVLA·NEC·MALIS

DIVOLSVS
QVERIMONIIS
SVPREMA·CITIVS
SOLVET·AMOR·DIE

From Time to Time, It Moves Around

BY LILY SUGRUE

Back in 1871, Dane Hall took a little trip around Harvard Yard. Harvard was building Matthews Hall at the time. Dane, the old law school, stood in the way, so the university moved the long-standing Greek Revival hall, Corinthian columns and all, forward toward the street and built the new Gothic structure right where its predecessor stood in the Yard.

Thirty years later Dane finally got some company at its new Massachusetts Avenue address. In 1901 two brick and wrought-iron gates were constructed near either side of the building. The gateways were designed by McKim, Mead & White as memorials for the classes of 1857 and 1875. The Class of 1875 Gate cost $4,665, equivalent to nearly $110,000 today.

The gate itself is a stoic creature, its outline heavy but not graceless. It is flanked at either end by thick, beveled brick posts; two Doric stone columns run down the middle and divide the entrance into three sections, with those on the outside slightly narrower than the central portion. Wrought-iron pickets decorated with spearheads fill these gaps, continuing the sense of power the gate exudes. The metal side panels are fixed to the gate, so only the central section allows pedestrians to pass through. It's a wonderful little trick.

By funneling all the pedestrians through one entrance, the architects have taken their imposing classical skeleton and made it a comfortable, person-sized walkway, friendly and inviting. The details are

understated but tasteful. Over the pediment, rounded stone ornaments sit where each pillar or post ends. Paneled brick walls, rather than fencing, extend out on either side of the gate.

Inscribed on the entablature facing Massachusetts Avenue is this quote from Isaiah 26:2: "Open Ye the Gates That the Righteous Nation Which Keepeth the Truth May Enter In." From the center of the entablature, a stone "Veritas" shield plumes upward. Harvard has left its calling card.

In 1918 Dane Hall went up in flames. By 1925 it had been replaced—Lehman Hall now stands on Dane's ashes. The 1875 and 1857 gates had to be moved and rearranged to adjust for the new building.

Unlike Dane before it, Lehman turns its back on the busy swirl of Harvard Square. The gate, in contrast, presents a welcoming face. Walk in. You never know. By the next time you make it back here, this all might have moved.

OVERLEAF: Two severe Doric columns subdivide the Class of 1875 Gate into three openings topped by successive layers of brick and limestone. The narrow side openings are fenced, funneling pedestrians through the wider central entry.

ACKNOWLEDGMENTS

A book, like a building, is not the work of one hand but of many, and so it is with *Gates of Harvard Yard*. Numerous people contributed their time and talents to this project, which began as a Wintersession class at Harvard University, became an e-book published by the Nieman Foundation for Journalism at Harvard, and culminated as a book published by Princeton Architectural Press.

Gates of Harvard Yard is built on a foundation laid by two Harvard scholars: Walter Dana Swan, whose critique, "The Harvard Memorial Gates," appeared in the *Architectural Review* in 1901; and Mason Hammond, whose article, "The Enclosure of the Harvard Yard," was published in the *Harvard Library Bulletin* in 1983. Along with Jeneen Interlandi and Finbarr O'Reilly, my fellow 2013 Nieman Fellows and valued coteachers of the Wintersession class, I repeatedly referred our students to these authoritative accounts.

We were directed to them and to other excellent sources by Barbara S. Meloni, the public services archivist at the Harvard University Library. Through her intelligence, diligence, and patience, Barbara made an indispensable contribution to this project. Harvard professors Alina Payne, Mark Laird, and Donald Pfister contributed expertise in their respective fields of Renaissance architecture, landscape architecture, and botany. *Harvard Gazette* staff writer Corydon Ireland made additional contributions by providing material about the gates.